Essential Question
In what ways can advances in science be helpful or harmful?

THE
BATTLE
AGAINST
PESTS

by Linda Bennett

CHAPTER 1

CONTROLLING PESTS

People started growing crops thousands of years ago. Since then, people have fought **pests** that attack crops. These pests are insects, weeds, and diseases.

People used different ways to keep pests away. People in ancient Greece sprayed their homes with sulfur to get rid of insects. In China, people used a poison called arsenic to keep garden pests away.

Ancient people grew their own food crops.

Pests can cause a lot of damage. In the 1200s, huge numbers of locusts covered the land in Egypt. The locusts ate and destroyed the crops.

In 1845, potato crops in Ireland got a disease called potato blight. The potatoes rotted in the ground. The potato blight caused a famine. Around 1 million people died because they had no food to eat.

Potatoes with blight have a terrible smell.

Crop rotation has helped keep pests away. Crops are rotated, or moved, into different fields each year. Diseases don't build up in the soil as easily. The soil can rest.

Scientists have also created pesticides to deal with pests. Pesticides are chemicals that kill pests. So, how did scientists **develop** pesticides? How well do they work?

STOP AND CHECK

How have people controlled pests?

Farmers spray pesticides to protect their crops.

CHAPTER 2

A CHEMICAL MIRACLE

In 1939, scientists discovered that a chemical called DDT killed insects. A pest called the Colorado potato beetle died when people sprayed DDT on it.

During World War II (1939–1945), lice were **prevalent**, or common, among soldiers. The soldiers became sick from a disease called typhus. Typhus was **spread**, or passed on, by lice. DDT killed lice. It helped keep typhus from spreading.

The Colorado potato beetle eats potato plants.

In the 1950s, DDT was sprayed on people to keep mosquitoes away.

Scientists worked to make other pesticides to protect crops against pests and disease. The scientists made further **advancements**. They made herbicides to kill weeds. They also developed crops that had **resistance** to herbicides. When farmers sprayed herbicides, the weeds died but the crops didn't.

Scientists also developed other insecticides to kill insect pests. These insecticides poisoned pests. They did not harm useful insects like bees. Bees help pollinate flowers.

Agriculture was changing at this time. Farms got larger. Farmers planted one or two kinds of crops instead of many kinds. They farmed in bigger fields. They used large machines. Farmers could grow and **harvest** more food.

Many farmers began using pesticides. A new machine sprayed chemicals over the crops as it drove through the fields. Some farmers sprayed DDT on crops.

STOP AND CHECK

How did modern pesticides develop?

Planes also sprayed pesticides on crops.

CHAPTER 3

PROTECTING THE ENVIRONMENT

Some people **disagreed** with the use of pesticides. They thought poisonous chemicals stayed on the food they ate.

Rachel Carson wrote a book called *Silent Spring* in 1962. Carson told how DDT harmed animals, birds, and people. It stayed in animals' bodies. It entered the **food web**. Carson also explained that DDT kills all insects, even the ones that are good for the environment.

People realized that DDT harmed the environment. Many people **protested** and spoke out against the use of DDT.

Carson changed people's ideas about pesticides. People wanted to know which pesticides were dangerous.

Carson's work led to the start of the Environmental Protection Agency (EPA) in 1970. The EPA protects our natural environment. It **banned** DDT in 1972. The chemical cannot be used in the United States anymore.

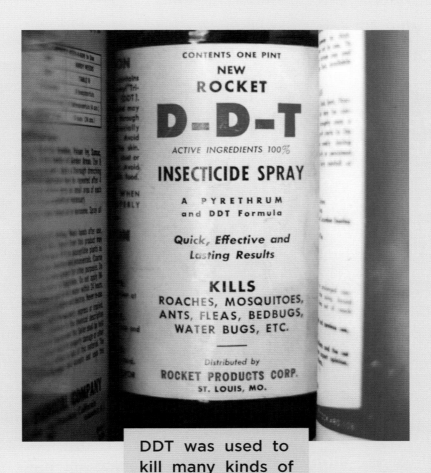

DDT was used to kill many kinds of insect pests.

The EPA still studies pesticides. It makes sure that pesticides don't harm people or the environment.

Environmental **activists** still worry about the dangers of pesticides. They tell people about their **concerns**.

STOP AND CHECK

Why did some people worry about using pesticides?

Spraying Apples

In 1986, scientists discovered that a pesticide called Alar caused cancer in rats. Alar was sprayed on apple trees. Many people stopped buying apples and apple juice. They worried that they might get cancer. Some farmers began growing apples without using pesticides. Alar is no longer used on food crops in the United States.

Many people fight against the use of pesticides.

Rich Pedroncelli/AP Images

CHAPTER 4
SAFE FOOD FOR THE FUTURE

Scientists are finding safe ways to protect crops. They develop plants with new **characteristics**. These plants aren't harmed by some

Some chrysanthemums naturally keep insects away.

diseases. Young plants **inherit** this resistance from the parent plants. As a result, these crops will be safe from disease.

Scientists look for helpful insects that eat insect pests. A tiny wasp helps control an insect called the corn borer. The wasp lays its eggs in the corn borers' eggs. This kills the corn borers' eggs.

Scientists also develop natural pesticides to keep insects away from plants. Natural pesticides wash off easily. They don't stay in the soil. **Organic** farms use natural pesticides.

The Pro-pesticide View

Farmers can use only pesticides that the government says are safe. Fruit that is grown using safe pesticides does not have bugs or disease.

Pesticides keep pests from destroying crops. Pesticides stop tragedies like the Irish potato famine from happening.

Pesticides are a cheap and easy way to protect our food resources. Pesticides make sure we have enough food for everyone.

Pesticides keep apples free of bugs.

The Anti-pesticide View

Organic farmers do not use pesticides, which pollute the environment. Organic famers control pests in natural ways. They use crop rotation. They use natural pesticides that don't harm the soil or crops. They use helpful insects.

Organic food is healthier than food grown with pesticides. Organic food is natural and safe.

Organic farms are safer and healthier places to work than farms that use pesticides. Workers don't breathe in poisonous sprays. Pesticides are bad for our health and our environment.

Organic farms grow many different crops.

The **population** of the world is growing every day. We need to have enough food to feed everyone in the world. So, farmers need to protect crops from pests. Our food also must be safe to eat.

We must produce enough food without harming the environment. Farmers, scientists, and communities can work together and make a healthy future for the whole planet.

STOP AND CHECK

How do farmers protect crops without using chemical pesticides?

14

Respond to Reading

Summarize

Use important details to summarize *The Battle Against Pests*. Your graphic organizer may help you.

Details

↓

Point of View

Text Evidence

1. What is the author's point of view about using pesticides? Give text evidence to support your answer. AUTHOR'S POINT OF VIEW

2. Find the word *rotated* on page 4. What does it mean? What clues in the text helped you figure it out? VOCABULARY

3. Write about the author's point of view about Rachel Carson and *Silent Spring* on pages 8-10. Use details from the text in your writing. WRITE ABOUT READING

Compare Texts
Read about how organic gardening deals with garden pests.

MAKING AN ORGANIC GARDEN

PREPARING YOUR GARDEN

Organic gardeners use natural ways to keep gardens healthy. Follow these steps to make an organic garden.

1. Mark out a small garden using string or stones.

2. Dig up the soil. (Always wear gloves.) Take out weeds. Look for earthworms. They dig tunnels in the soil. These tunnels allow air and water to reach a plant's roots.

3. Mix in some compost. You can make compost from fallen leaves, grass clippings, and vegetable peelings.

Earthworms help make compost.

PLANTING YOUR GARDEN

Now you are ready to plant. Plant organic seeds or seedlings. Leave enough space between the plants or seeds.

Choose some plants to keep insect pests away. Garlic drives away the Japanese beetle. Cilantro keeps away aphids and white flies.

Some plants attract helpful insects. Ladybugs eat pests called aphids. Aphids feed on the leaves of plants.

Ladybugs keep plants free from pests.

TAKING CARE OF YOUR GARDEN

Weed your garden often. Pull out the whole weed. The weed will grow back if the root is left behind.

You can make natural sprays to drive away harmful pests. Spraying salt and warm water keeps away caterpillars and cabbage worms.

Organic gardening is fun and good for the planet, too.

It's fun to grow vegetables.

Ariel Skelley/Blend Images/Getty Images

Make Connections

How do organic gardeners keep their gardens healthy? ESSENTIAL QUESTION

Compare organic methods to grow plants with the methods that use pesticides. TEXT TO TEXT

Glossary

activists *(AK-ti-vists)* people who take political action *(page 10)*

food web *(fewd web)* the system of living things in an environment that depend on each other for food *(page 8)*

harvest *(HAHR-vuhst)* to gather in a crop when it is ready *(page 7)*

organic *(or-GA-nik)* natural; not using chemicals *(page 11)*

Index

Focus on Science

Purpose To show the good and bad effects of pesticides

Procedure

Step 1 Work with a partner or small group. Research the good effects and the bad effects of a pesticide that is used today.

Step 2 Talk about what you found out with your partner or group. Make a list in two columns. List the good effects about using the pesticide in one column. List the bad effects about using the pesticide in the other column.

Step 3 Present your list to the class. Describe the good effects and the bad effects of using the pesticide.

Conclusion After listening to the good effects and the bad effects of using the different pesticides, are you for or against using pesticides?